MW00886763

SPACE
ACTIVITY BOOK

FOR 5-7 YEAR OLDS

THIS BOOK BELONGS TO:

Receive a FREE gift!

Go to our website and download for free the printable tracing book.

smartlittleowl.com/gift

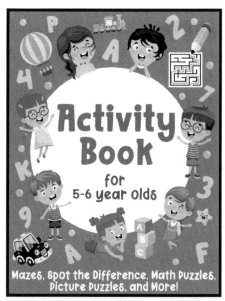

Activity Book for 5-6 year olds

Mazes, Spot the Difference, Math Puzzles, Picture Puzzles, and More!

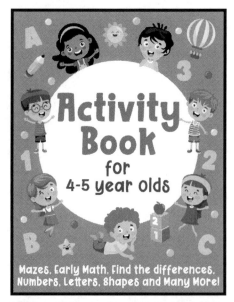

Activity Book for 4-5 year olds

Mazes, Early Math, Find the differences, Numbers, Letters, Shapes and Many More!

WORD SEARCH for kids Ages 5-7

A fun and enjoyable way to improve letter recognition, spelling skills and vocabulary

Activity Book for 3-4 year olds

Spot the difference, mazes, math puzzles, picture puzzles, numbers, letters, and more!

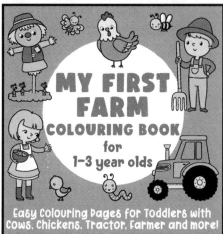

MY FIRST FARM COLOURING BOOK for 1-3 year olds

Easy Colouring Pages for Toddlers with Cows, Chickens, Tractor, Farmer and more!

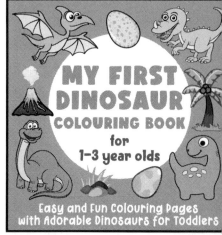

MY FIRST DINOSAUR COLOURING BOOK for 1-3 year olds

Easy and Fun Colouring Pages with Adorable Dinosaurs for Toddlers

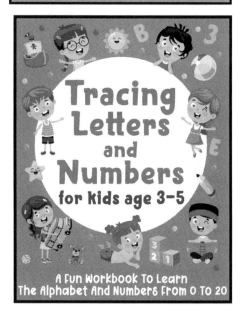

Tracing Letters and Numbers for kids age 3-5

A Fun Workbook To Learn The Alphabet And Numbers From 0 To 20

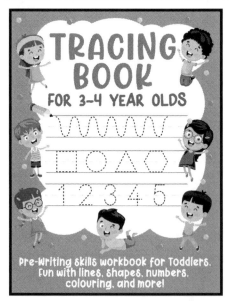

TRACING BOOK FOR 3-4 YEAR OLDS

Pre-Writing skills workbook for Toddlers. Fun with lines, shapes, numbers, colouring, and more!

Prewriting Skills Workbook for toddlers

Fun pen control and tracing for 3 year olds

SEE MORE OF OUR PRODUCTS

Books ▾ | smart little owl

Find the right path.

1

WORD SEARCH

```
M S U N M Y Q P A
C T F M A R S C S
B A R X K P Q O T
M R O C K E T M R
F D R N O S A E O
G R B C K X M T N
T M I S S I O N A
Q R T N R O O R U
Z A S M T P N B T
```

ASTRONAUT	MISSION	ROCKET
COMET	MOON	STAR
MARS	ORBIT	SUN

2

Find the right path.

Find the sun among the planets.

Count how many rockets are in each box and write the correct number.

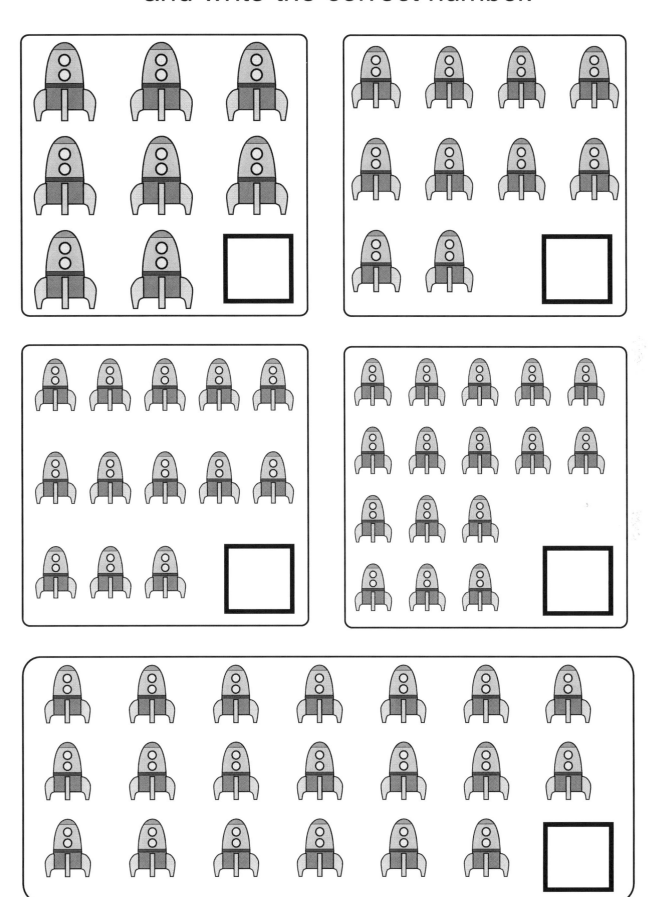

Find the right path.

Find 6 differences.

Count and write how many.

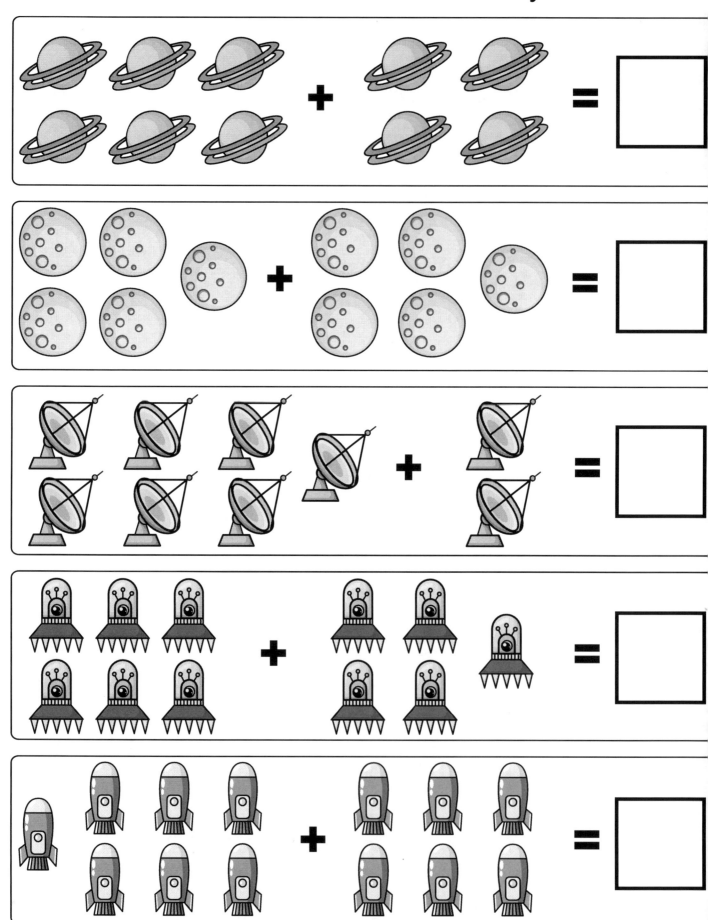

Find two identical satellites.

Find the right path.

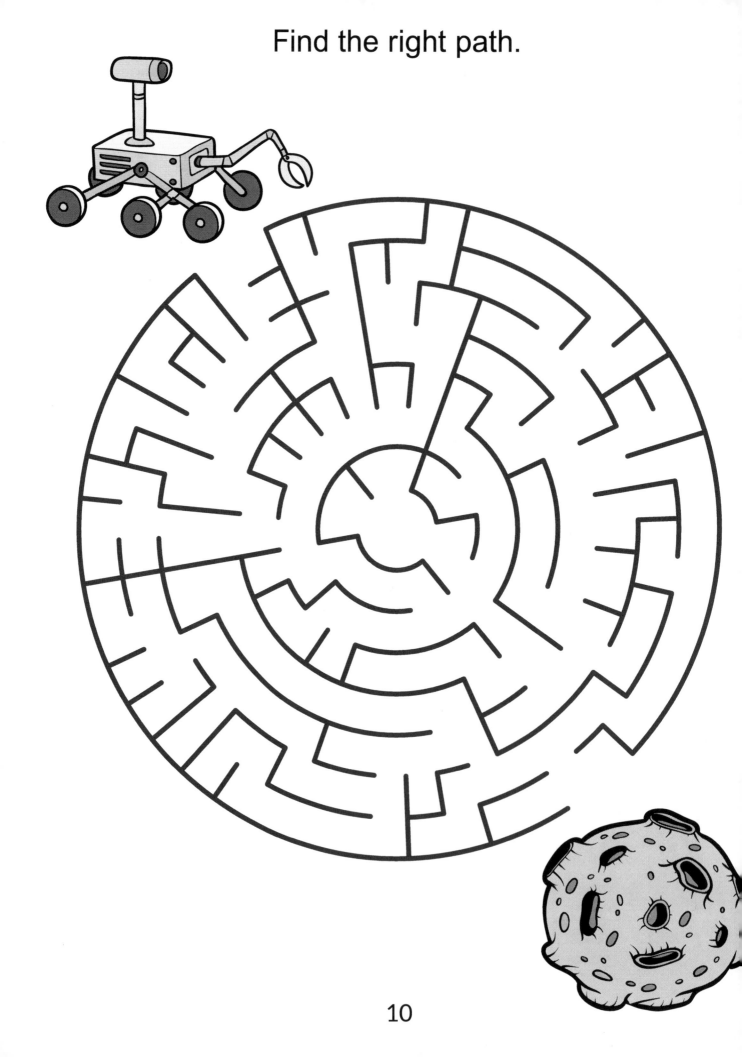

Cross out 3 things. Count how many are left. Write the number in the box.

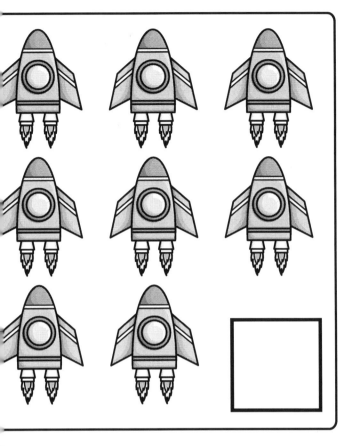

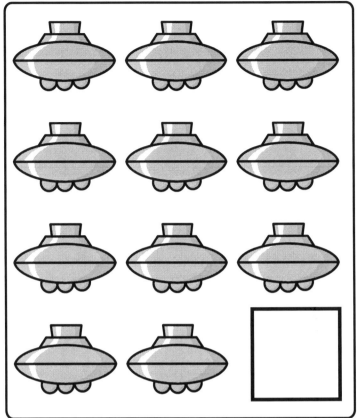

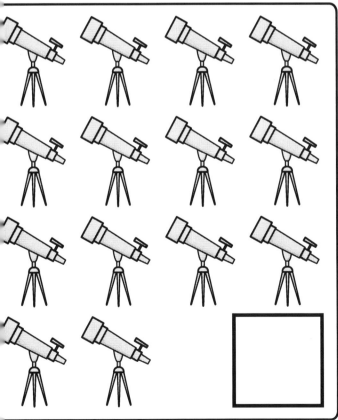

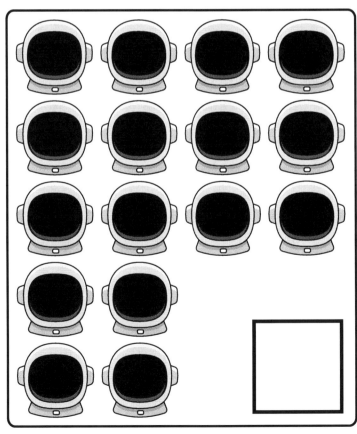

Find the right path.

Circle the picture that is different than the rest.

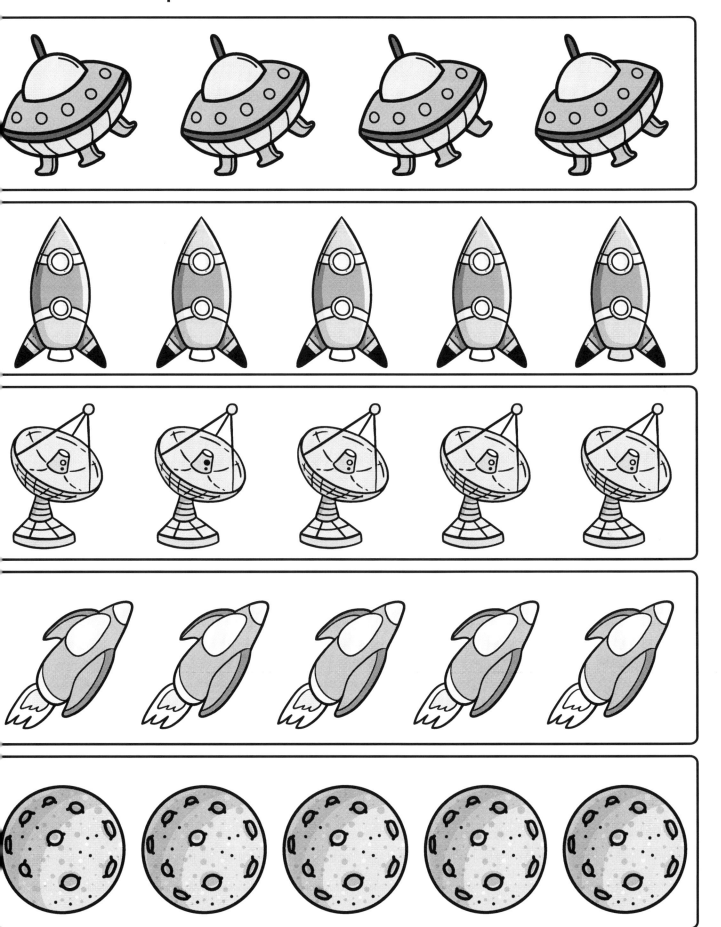

Can you unscramble the words below?

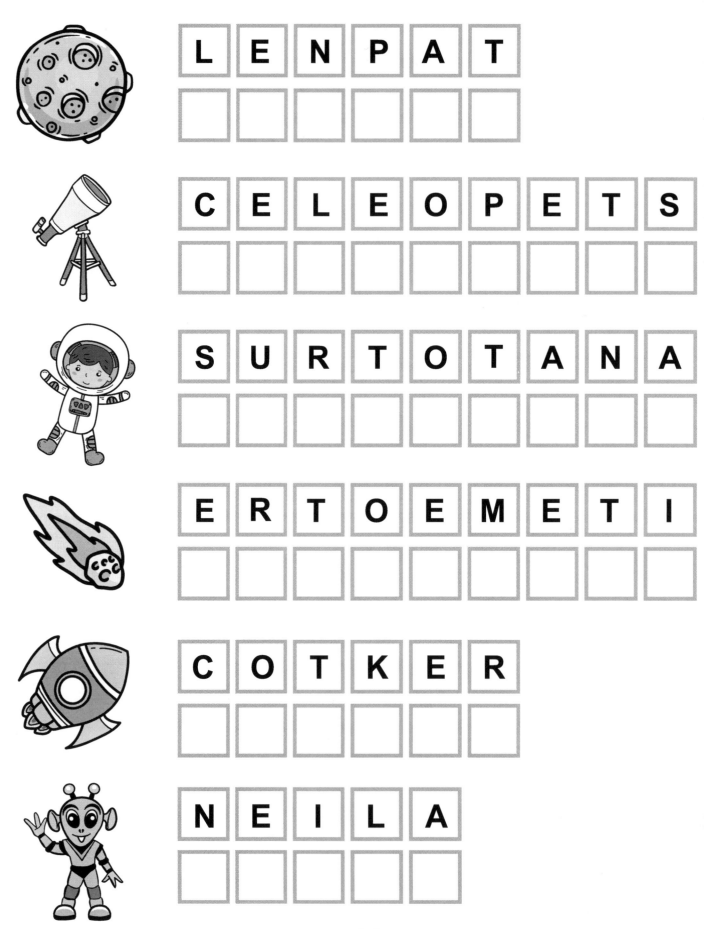

L E N P A T

C E L E O P E T S

S U R T O T A N A

E R T O E M E T I

C O T K E R

N E I L A

Find 6 differences.

Count and write how many.

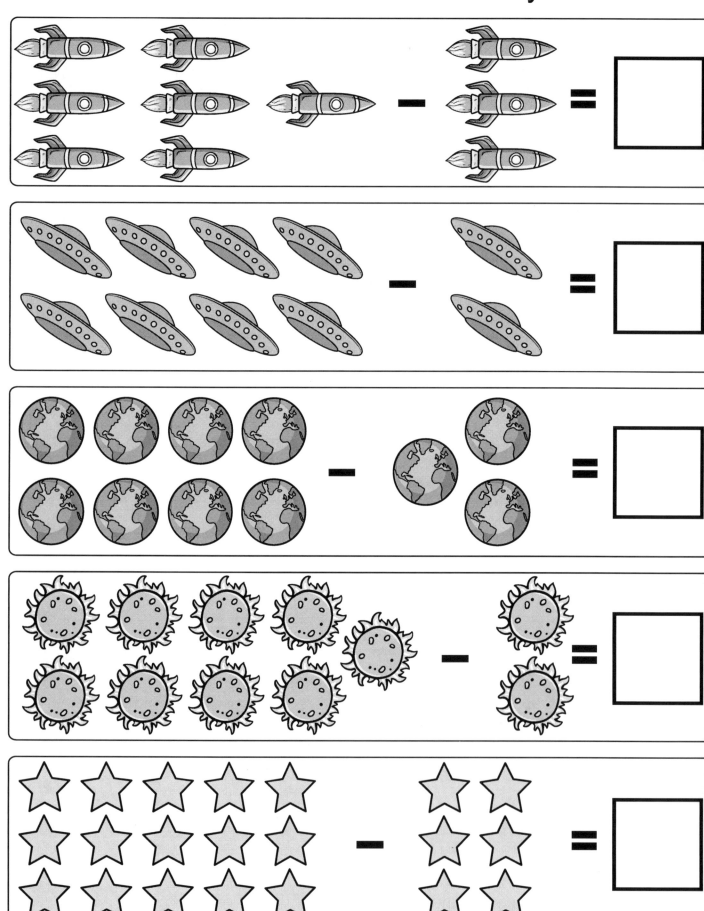

Find the right path.

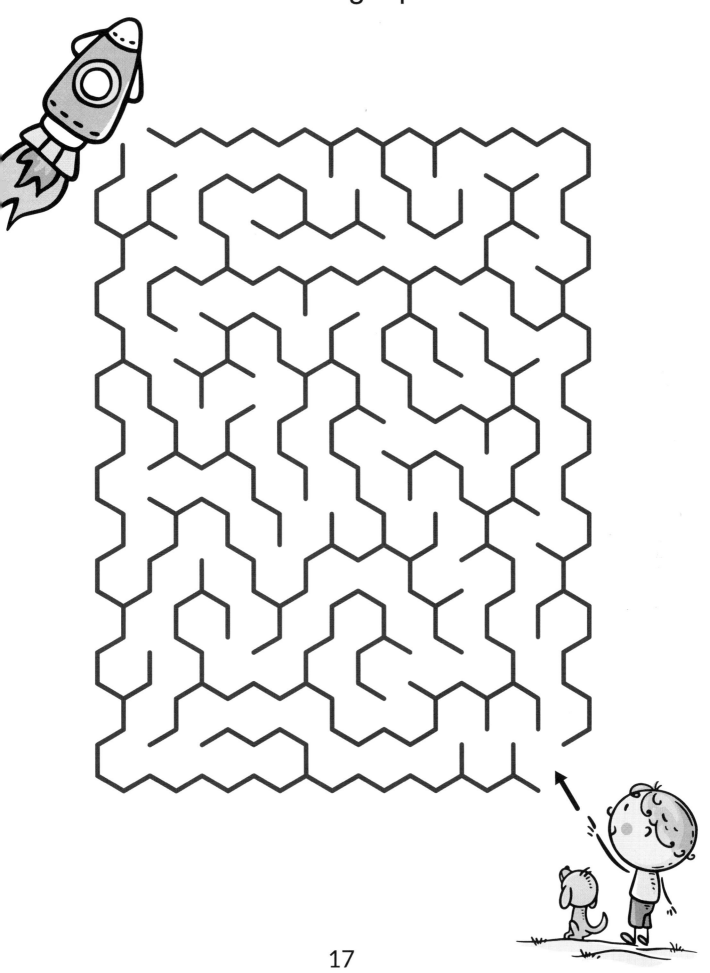

Complete the picture.

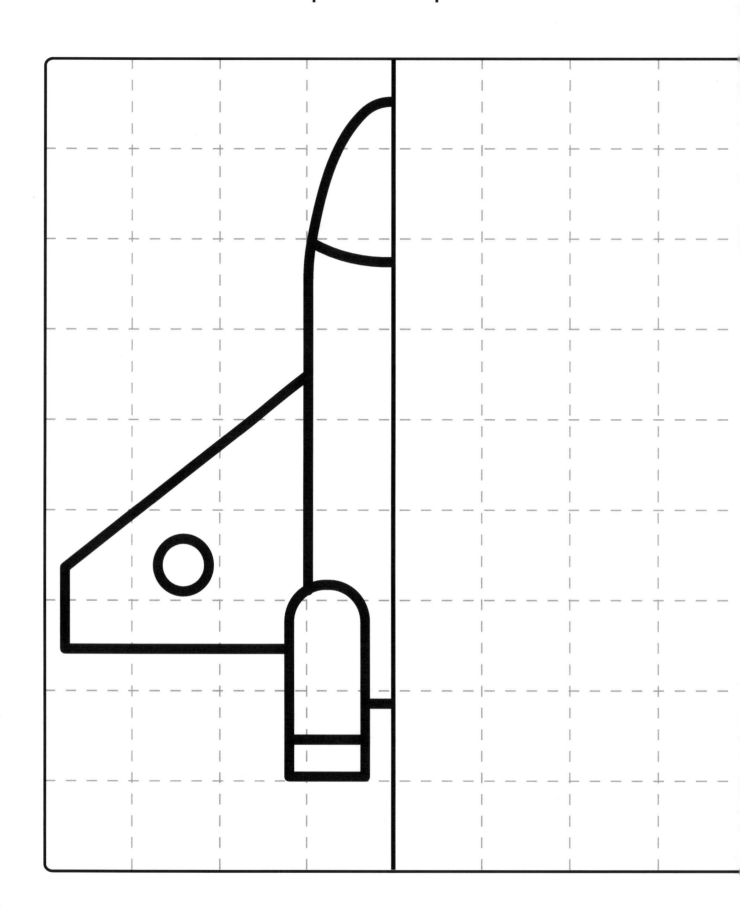

WORD SEARCH

```
S A T U R N Q P V
P J E A R T H L E
A U C X K P Q A N
C P L Q R N T N U
E I I N Z S A E S
G T P C K X P T N
T E S T C J L P X
Q R E M E T E O R
G A L A X Y N B T
```

EARTH	JUPITER	SATURN
ECLIPSE	METEOR	SPACE
GALAXY	PLANET	VENUS

Find the right path.

Write the numbers in order from least to greatest.

One of these astronauts doesn't have a twin. Which one is it?

Find the right path.

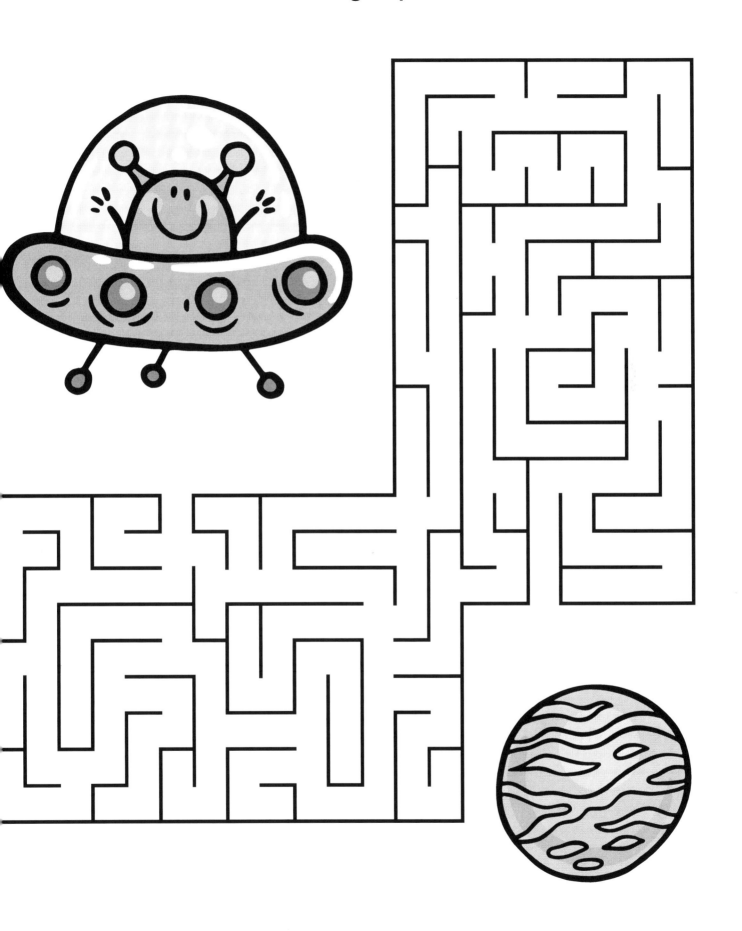

There is one rocket that is different. Find it.

Find the right path.

Find 7 differences.

Find the right path.

27

Copy the picture.

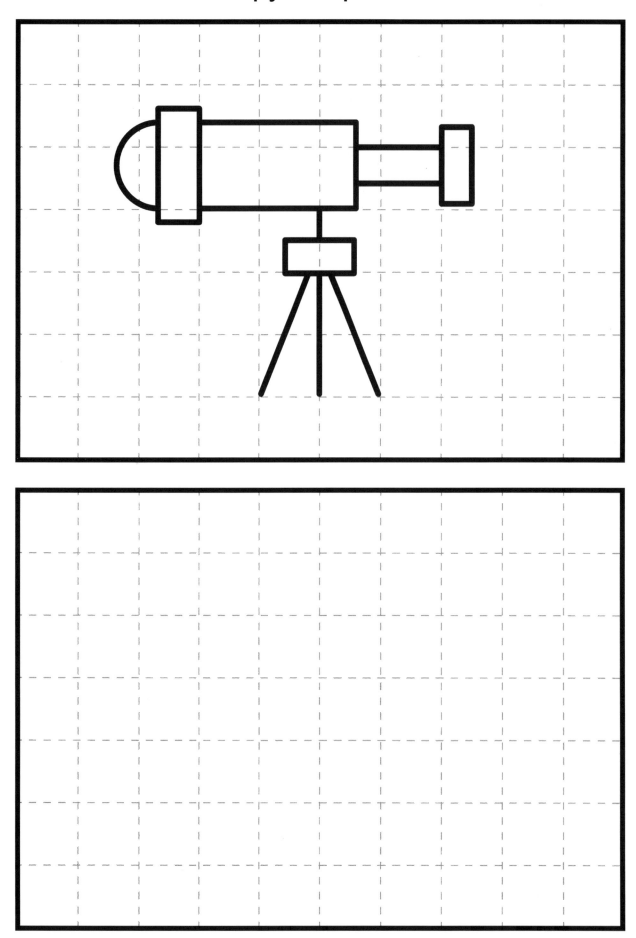

Find the right path.

Fill in the missing numbers.

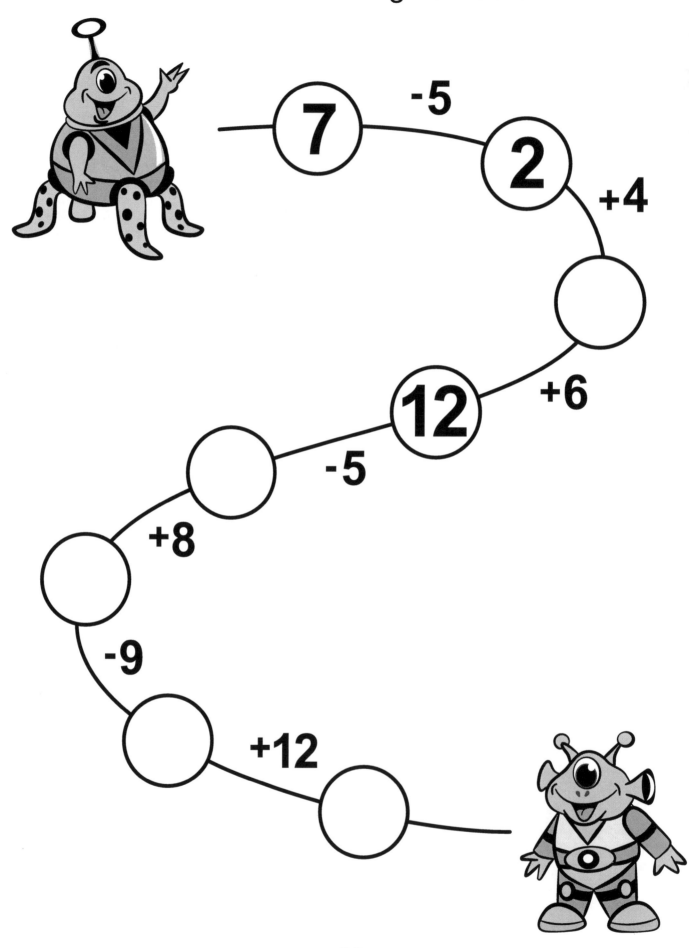

7 −5 2 +4 ◯ +6 12 −5 ◯ +8 ◯ −9 ◯ +12 ◯

Find the right path.

Look at the order of the pictures.
Then draw the rest to finish each row.

Find the right path.

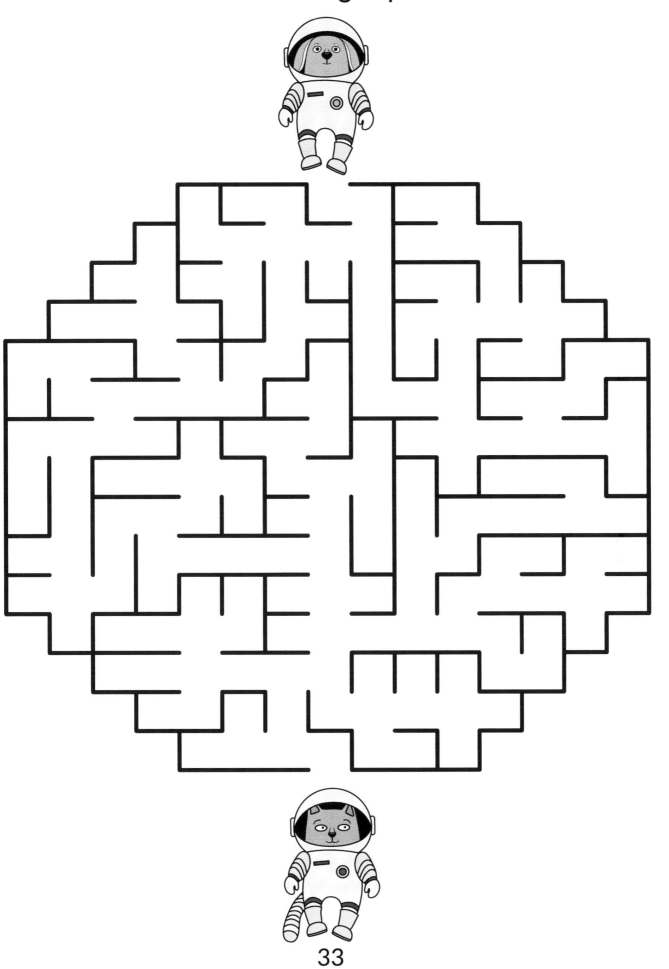

WORD SEARCH

```
L A U N C H S S A
A W T B A S H P U
S U A X P I U A N
T P L C S R T C I
E T I N U I T E V
R M E C L U L S E
O N N S E S E H R
I Z R Q T M N I S
D A S O L A R P E
```

ALIEN   LAUNCH   SOLAR

ASTEROID   SHUTTLE   SPACESHIP

CAPSULE   SIRIUS   UNIVERSE

Score a total of 20 points to help the astronaut get to the rocket.

3

2

1

2

2

2

3

2

1

2

4

2

2

4

2

4

2

1

2

3

3

2

Write ⊕ or ⊖ to complete equations.

8 ☐ 4 = 12		15 ☐ 3 = 12
14 ☐ 4 = 10		16 ☐ 2 = 18
13 ☐ 2 = 15		11 ☐ 4 = 15
10 ☐ 4 = 6		15 ☐ 5 = 10
12 ☐ 3 = 15		10 ☐ 5 = 5
11 ☐ 4 = 7		13 ☐ 3 = 10
12 ☐ 3 = 9		10 ☐ 7 = 17

Find the right path.

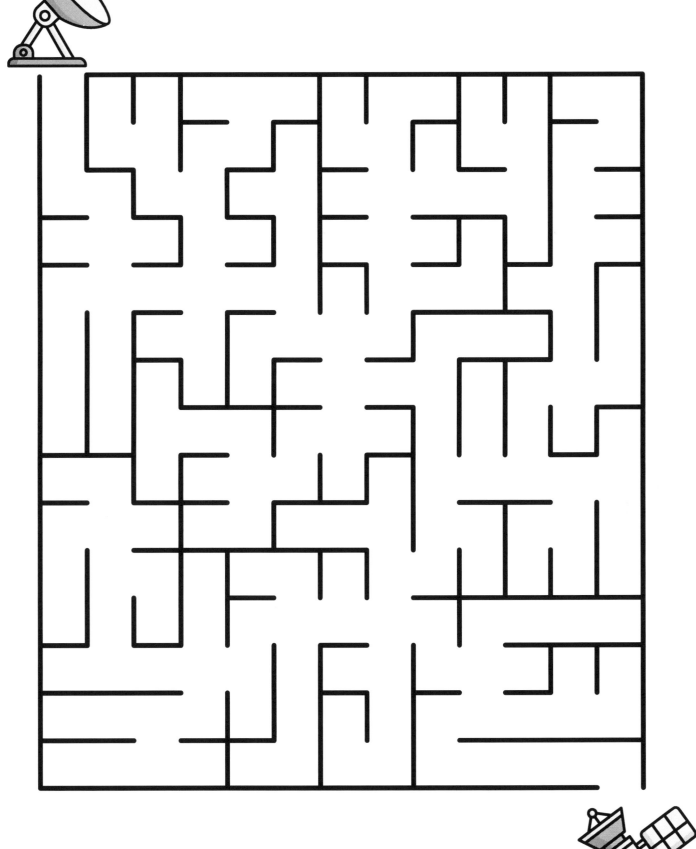

Find 7 differences.

Find the right path.

Write the missing numbers.

5 + ⬚ = 10 - ⬚ = 8 +

⬚ = 11 - ⬚ = 5 +

+   9

3   ⬚ = 4   =   -

=   -   12

13   -   =

-    =   + 10 =   6

7   +

=   ⬚ + 1 =   ⬚ - 6 = ⬚

Find the right path.

Connect the dots.

Find the right path.

Can you unscramble the words below?

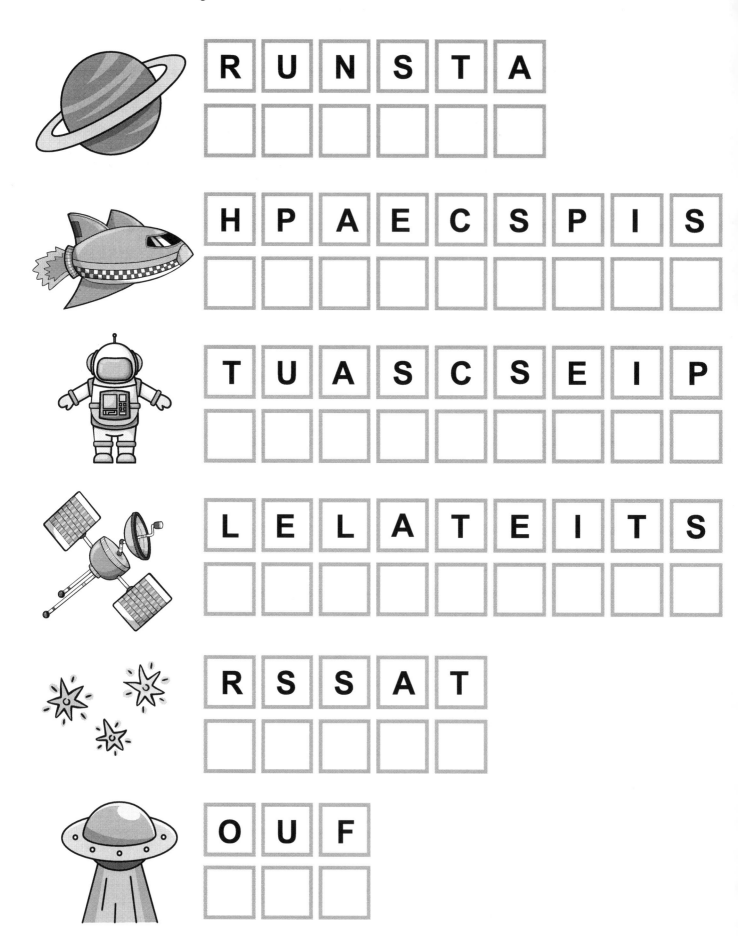

R U N S T A

H P A E C S P I S

T U A S C S E I P

L E L A T E I T S

R S S A T

O U F

44

Find the right path.

WORD SEARCH

```
S T E L L A R G T
U P N D M L G R E
P R C P E U Q A L
E F X L R R Z V E
R K M U C A X I S
N E P T U N E T C
O E S O R U O Y O
V R N M Y S P Q P
A O N E B U L A E
```

GRAVITY	NEPTUNE	SUPERNOVA
MERCURY	PLUTO	TELESCOPE
NEBULA	STELLAR	URANUS

Find the right path.

Find 7 differences.

Find the right path.

Write the numbers in order from greatest to least.

Find the right path.

Can you help the astronaut get to the spaceship? Draw a path from the astronaut to the spaceship by counting from 1 to 20.

	→ 1	2	5	6
	4	3	4	7
13	12	11	10	9	8
14	17	13	8	11	10
15	12	15	20 →		
16	17	18	19		

Fill in the missing numbers.

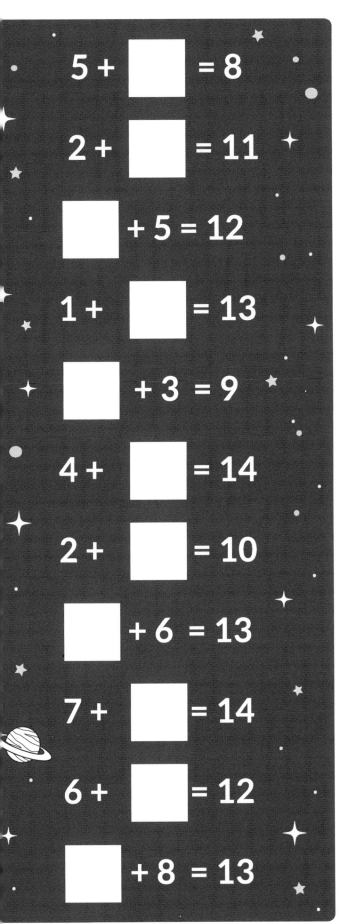

5 + ⬜ = 8

2 + ⬜ = 11

⬜ + 5 = 12

1 + ⬜ = 13

⬜ + 3 = 9

4 + ⬜ = 14

2 + ⬜ = 10

⬜ + 6 = 13

7 + ⬜ = 14

6 + ⬜ = 12

⬜ + 8 = 13

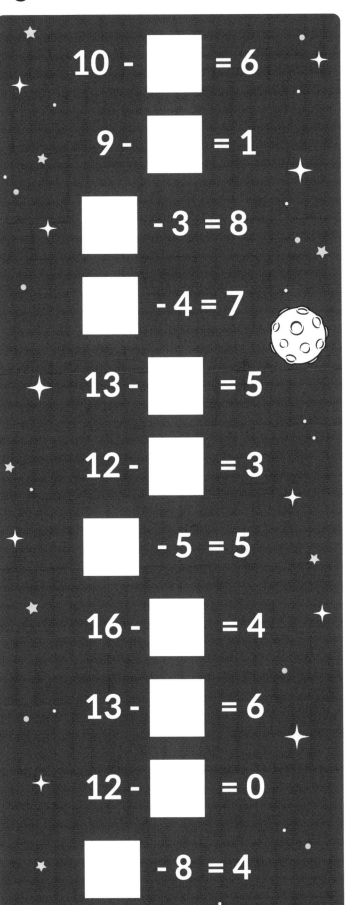

10 - ⬜ = 6

9 - ⬜ = 1

⬜ - 3 = 8

⬜ - 4 = 7

13 - ⬜ = 5

12 - ⬜ = 3

⬜ - 5 = 5

16 - ⬜ = 4

13 - ⬜ = 6

12 - ⬜ = 0

⬜ - 8 = 4

53

Find the right path.

Find 8 differences.

Follow the steps below to learn how to draw a rocket

1.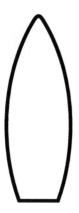

2.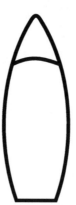

3.

4.

5.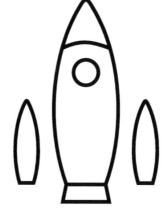

6.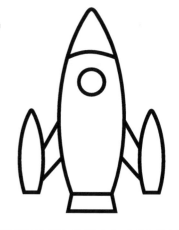

Find the right path.

57

WORD SEARCH

```
S L A N D I N G E
A H M D E L G C X
T C C P B U Q O P
E R L A O R A S L
L A A R R A S M O
L E P O P C T I R
I S S R R U R C E
T E N U Y S A E P
E R N A B U L A W
```

ASTRAL   AURORA   COSMIC

CREW   EXPLORE   LANDING

PROBE   RESEARCH   SATELLITE

Find the right path.

Connect the dots.

Find the right path.

ANSWER KEY

Page 1

Page 2

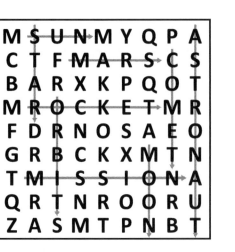

Page 3

Page 4

Page 5

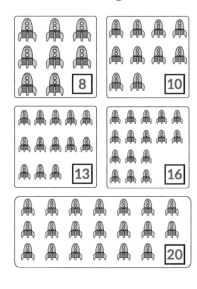

Page 6

Page 7

Page 8

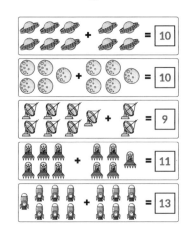

Page 9

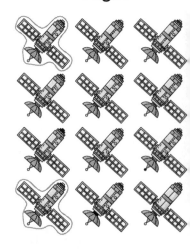

ANSWER KEY

Page 10

Page 11

5

8

11

13

Page 12

Page 13

Page 14

L	E	N	P	A	T		
P	L	A	N	E	T		

C	E	L	E	O	P	E	T	S
T	E	L	E	S	C	O	P	E

S	U	R	T	O	T	A	N	A
A	S	T	R	O	N	A	U	T

E	R	T	O	E	M	E	T	I
M	E	T	E	O	R	I	T	E

C	O	T	K	E	R			
R	O	C	K	E	T			

N	E	I	L	A				
A	L	I	E	N				

Page 15

Page 16

– = 4

– = 6

– = 5

– = 7

– = 9

Page 17

Page 18

63

ANSWER KEY

Page 19

Page 20

Page 21

Page 22

Page 23

Page 24

Page 25

Page 26

Page 27

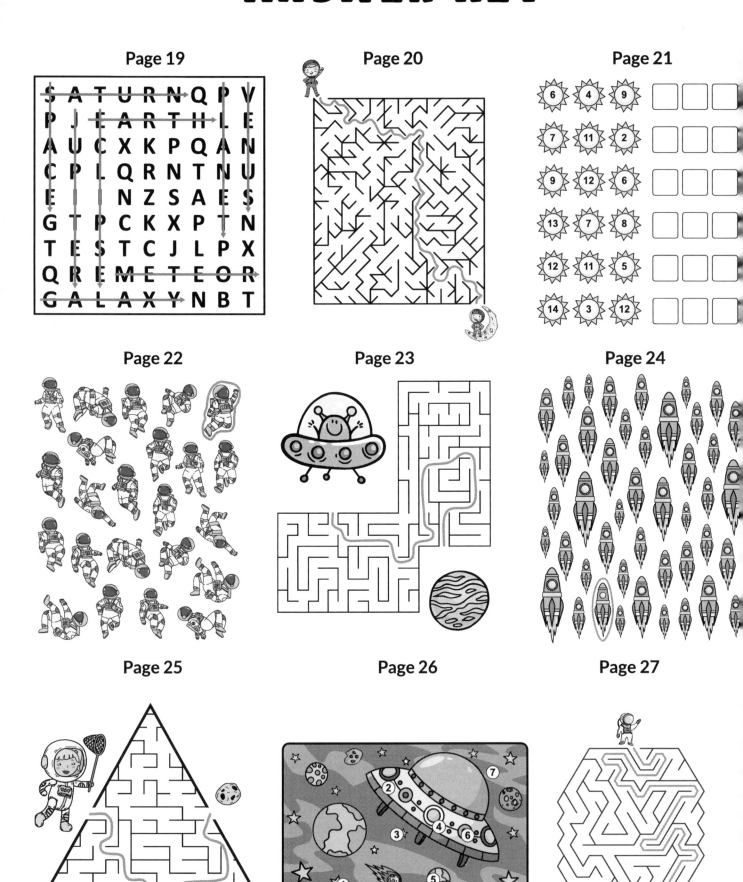

ANSWER KEY

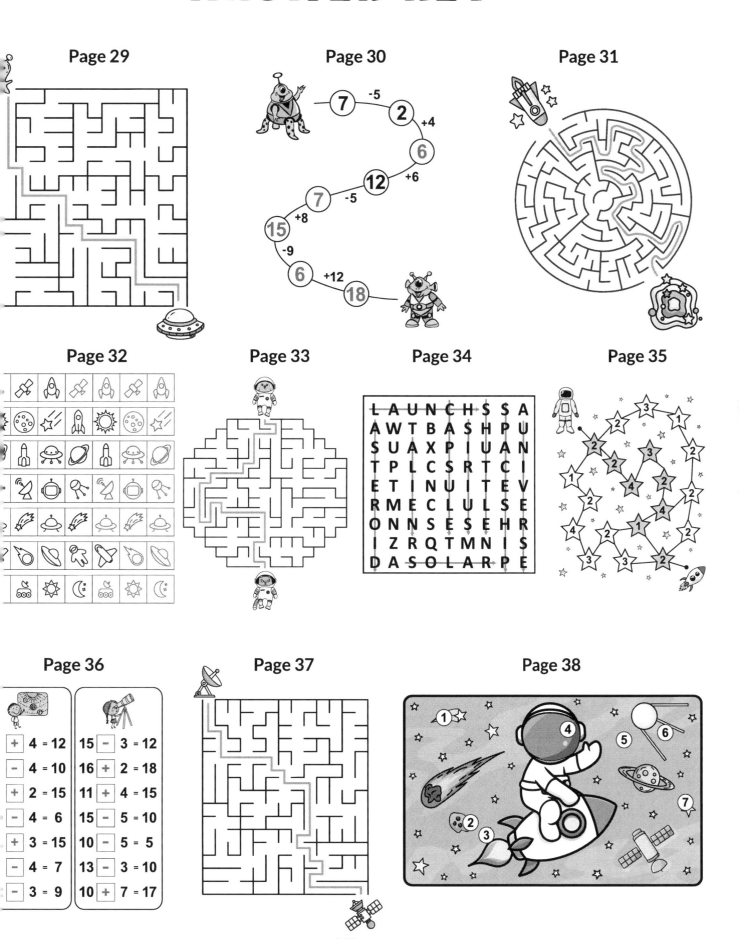

Page 29

Page 30

7 -5 2 +4 6 +6 12 -5 7 +8 15 -9 6 +12 18

Page 31

Page 32

Page 33

Page 34

L A U N C H S S A
A W T B A S H P U
S U A X P I U A N
T P L C S R T C I
E T I N U I T E V
R M E C L U L S E
O N N S E S E H R
I Z R Q T M N I S
D A S O L A R P E

Page 35

Page 36

+	4	= 12	15	−	3	= 12
−	4	= 10	16	+	2	= 18
+	2	= 15	11	+	4	= 15
−	4	= 6	15	−	5	= 10
+	3	= 15	10	−	5	= 5
−	4	= 7	13	−	3	= 10
−	3	= 9	10	+	7	= 17

Page 37

Page 38

ANSWER KEY

Page 39

Page 40

5	+	5	=	10	-	2	=	8	+

							1
8	=	11	-	6	=	5	+
							=
+		9	=	4		7	9
3							-
=		-			12		3
4		13				-	=
-		=	3	+	10	=	2	6
7							+
=	6	+	1	=	5	-	6	=	0

Page 41

Page 42

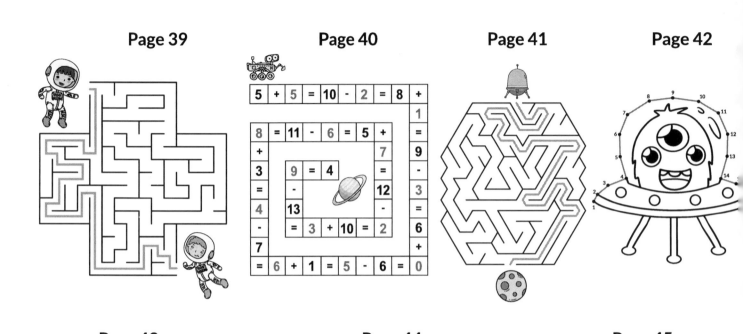

Page 43

Page 44

R U N S T A
S A T U R N

H P A E C S P I
S P A C E S H I

T U R S C S E I
S P A C E S U I

L E B A T E I T
S A E E L L I T

R S S A T
S T A R S

O U F
U F O

Page 45

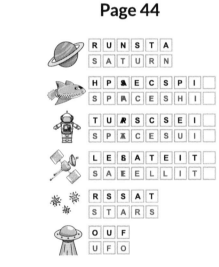

Page 46

S	T	E	L	L	A	R	G	T
U	P	N	D	M	L	G	R	E
P	R	C	P	E	U	Q	A	L
E	F	X	L	R	R	Z	V	E
R	K	M	U	C	A	X	I	S
N	E	P	T	U	N	E	T	C
O	E	S	O	R	U	O	Y	O
V	R	N	M	Y	S	P	Q	P
A	O	N	E	B	U	L	A	E

Page 47

Page 48

66

ANSWER KEY

Page 49

Page 50

7 5 9	9	7	5
8 11 15	15	11	8
9 8 12	12	9	8
13 14 11	14	13	11
12 1 11	12	11	1
13 15 14	15	14	13

Page 51

Page 52

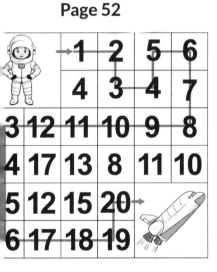

1	2	5	6
4	3	4	7
12	11	10	9	8
17	13	8	11	10
12	15	20
17	18	19

Page 53

5 + 3 = 8	10 - 4 = 6
2 + 9 = 11	9 - 8 = 1
7 + 5 = 12	11 - 3 = 8
1 + 11 = 13	11 - 4 = 7
6 + 3 = 9	13 - 8 = 5
4 + 10 = 14	12 - 9 = 3
2 + 8 = 10	10 - 5 = 5
7 + 6 = 13	16 - 12 = 4
7 + 7 = 14	13 - 7 = 6
6 + 6 = 12	12 - 12 = 0
5 + 8 = 13	12 - 8 = 4

Page 54

Page 55

Page 57

Page 58

S	L	A	N	D	I	N	G	E
A	H	M	D	E	L	G	C	X
T	C	C	P	B	U	Q	O	P
E	R	L	A	O	R	A	S	L
L	A	A	R	R	A	S	M	O
L	E	P	O	P	C	T	I	R
I	S	S	R	R	U	R	C	E
T	E	N	U	Y	S	A	E	P
E	R	N	A	B	U	L	A	W

ANSWER KEY

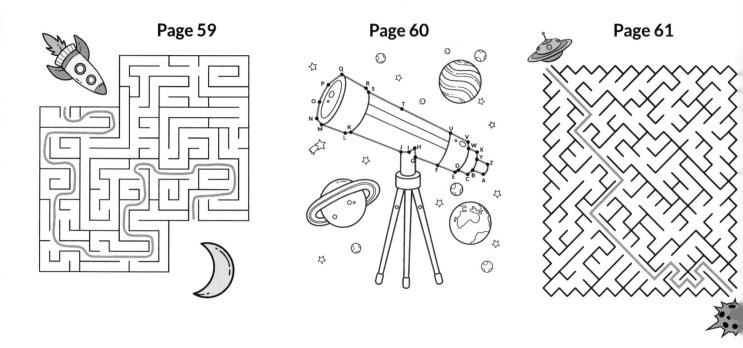

Page 59

Page 60

Page 61

Made in United States
Orlando, FL
18 July 2024

49138111R00039